To: _Cam & Jeff_

From: _Grandpa & Grandma_

Date: _December 25, 2014_

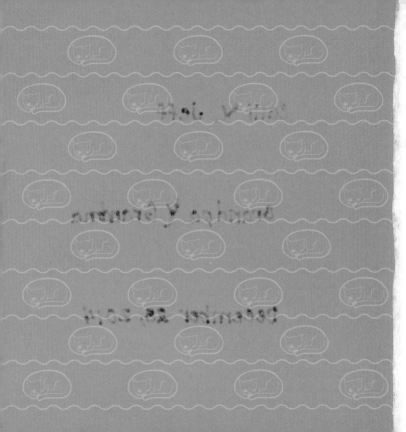

I'D RATHER BE A CAT

By Allia Zobel Nolan

HARVEST HOUSE PUBLISHERS

EUGENE, OREGON

I'D RATHER BE A CAT

Text Copyright © 2012 by Allia Zobel Nolan
Photos compiled by Allia Zobel Nolan

All photos, except for pages 24 and 27, from Shutterstock.com
Photos on page 24 and 27 from BigStock

Published by Harvest House Publishers
Eugene, Oregon 97402
www.harvesthousepublishers.com

ISBN 978-0-7369-3934-8

Design and production by Mary pat Design, Westport, Connecticut

For more information about Allia Zobel Nolan, visit her at:
www.AlliaWrites.com
www.kittyliterate.blogspot.com
www.theworrywartsprayerbook.wordpress.com

Printed in China
12 13 14 15 16 17 18 / LP / 10 9 8 7 6 5 4 3 2 1

I dedicate this book to God, who made all the animals special but in my opinion, took more time with cats than dogs; to my husband, Desmond, who, with much patience and love, tolerates the "kit-tehs" and has always longed for a floppy-eared animal who barks and comes when he's called; and to my three furry children, Angela Dah-ling, MacDuff, and Sineady-Cat-the-Fraidy-Cat, who demonstrate every day in every way that they are, paws down and far and away, above the pack.

—Allia Zobel Nolan

Every dog wants to be me. Isn't it obvious why? I mean, look at me! Awesome, right? There's just no contest-o, Fido. Cats have dogs licked. Period!

THE PURR-FECT ANSWER

It's a controversial question: Which companion animal is better, the cat or the dog?

"Ask the animals themselves," my muse whispered.

I took her advice and dug up a secret so astounding that it could change the way we look at these animals forever. Apparently, while cats have no doubts they're not just *better* but the *best,* our canine friends are not so confident.

I talked with one stuttering whistle-blower who could hardly get the words out. "A great many of us—and I'm not naming names—well, we actually believe… We believe…cats are better. And if we had our druthers, we'd… Well, we'd…rather be cats! There, I've said it!"

So now, even dogs concede that puddies *are* paramount. However, to quiet any naysayers, I queried a clowder of felines as to *why* they'd rather be a cat. The response was overwhelming. What follows are some—but by no means all—of the answers from cats around the globe.

Oh, and one more thing—you'll see that whereas dogs admittedly envy cats for their many positive qualities, cats most definitely don't return the sentiment.

—Allia Zobel Nolan

WE ARE CAT.

We don't have self-esteem issues. We don't look to our humans for approval. We don't jump all over them to seek acceptance.

Nobody uses the word "cat" in a derogatory manner. But, when something's considered unattractive, what do humans call it? You got it—a "dog."

Cats are ecological. We don't waste energy on banalities such as fetching or shaking hands. An order to sit or roll over? Fuhgetaboutit!

Though we'd prefer
they stay at home,
our humans *could* go
away for a weekend
without putting
us in expensive
boardinghouses.
But why would they
want to?

Cats are not at anyone's beck and call. However, if you open a can of sardines, we just might appear out of nowhere.

Cats are generous. We're only too eager to share delicacies—like mice, garden snakes, and moths—with our humans.

Unlike dogs, who fidget
uncontrollably, you'd never
know a cat was in the room
unless, heaven forbid, you
step on her tail.

We cats don't beg. It's not our style. We simply put on our if-I-don't-get-a-treat-this-second-I'll-die face. See? Then *everything* is ours.

Cats hunt alone—never with a human. We don't chase foxes. And we don't retrieve anything for anyone.

Unlike dogs, cats don't run in packs. We make discerning friendships and are fiercely loyal to our BFFs (Best Friends Fur-ever).

You'll never have to douse us with tomato juice because we're smart enough to know that skunks are not to be trifled with. Duh!

We could roll over, jump through fire, or catch Frisbees. But, well, why bother?

Dogs are known for their annoying trait—barking. Cats are recognized for the sweetest sound on earth—purring.

Cats don't subscribe to the
anything-that-drops-on-the-
floor-is-mine food approach.
We exhibit flawless table etiquette
and never gobble our meals.

A cat's breath
does not smell
like a mixture of a
dumpster and an
old locker.

Cats like us are super respectful of our human's visitors. We would never cling to a guest's leg, nor would we ever salivate on them.

Okay, so we might stick our heads in the whipped-cream bowl…just out of curiosity. But roll in the mud? Ewww! Gross!

Cats are intuitive thinkers.
We weigh our options
before we pounce, if, in
fact, we pounce at all.

Unlike dogs, who are set in their ways, cats are never afraid to try new things.

Chase our tails? Oh, pa-leese. We cats certainly run in the *right* circles, but never *aimlessly around* in circles like a you-know-who does.

Though we have excellent
voices and might occasionally
croon a love song to our
mates, cats would never howl
at the moon.

You never have to bathe a cat. We're self-cleaning.

Slander mongers say we're aloof and snooty because we don't come when we are called. Not so. Cats just know how to turn a deaf ear when we're not interested.

Cats are peace loving. We would never use aggression to get our point across nor bare our teeth— unless we are yawning.

Our humans never have to waste time taking us for walks to the powder room, nor will they have to carry suspicious plastic bags back home afterward.

Cats have impeccable comportment. We exude civility and have the best manners. We never dribble, nor do we ever drool.

We're seldom in a hurry. We can stare at a spider for hours or until Mom screams and it runs away.

Unlike our hyper canine counterparts, cats are patient and full of restraint.

We think about things
before we make a move.

Cats are individualists—
independent thinkers
who are not influenced
by the crowd. We are not
interested in anyone's
opinion but our own.

Okay! Okay, Fido, let's try it again. If you want to be a cat, you've got to be more aloof. Be calm. Be cool. Be controlled. Yes, I think you're swell too. Now GET OFF OF ME!